SPEED SYSTEMS

Why You Go Faster

Edition 05

FOLLOWGOD ABOVE

DEDICATION

This book is dedicated to
FRIENDS AND PARTNERS
of APOSTLE FOLLOWGOD ABOVE

TABLE OF CONTENTS

SPEED SYSTEMS

Time is so short yet so much needs to be done. Every century witnesses a decline in human life-span, but this fact has not translated to a reduced workload rather more and more tasks beckon. The coming of the Lord is sooner than ever while global soul harvest is still an enormous task. No man really has enough time for his overwhelming destiny exploits. What do you do when you have very limited time to execute a mountain of work?

The Bible says,

And there are also many other things which Jesus did, the which, if they should be written every one, I suppose that even the world itself could not contain the books that should be written. Amen.

John 21:25

Let us think for a minute: a man is born with a mandate to do great exploits, the record of which the world would not contain, but has only three and half years to complete his task. What do you think would be the approach of such a man to work? Slow but steady? Any man that understands the magnitude of his divine assignment and the very brief time he has for its realization will never be slothful in business. Speed is a necessity. If you must realize your destiny, you do not just need to be fast, you need to be very, very fast.

Whatsoever God destined you to do, you need to do it very quickly. King David said, "...the king's business required haste" (1 Sam. 21:8). The truth is, speed is more required now than ever—you need to be faster in your destiny-realizing efforts than those who lived in the past millennia. The era of "slow but steady" is long gone. No man can run with the pace of a snail and cope in this speed-conscious age. The emphasis worldwide is on excellence and speed.

People want the best answer the next second. People want excellent result at the speed of light. The world is increasingly impatient with mediocrity and delay and you need to have excellence and speed as your success-benchmarks. Globally, products that are efficient sell better. For this reason, manufacturers are doing all manner of product upgrading to remain competitive in the market. It is the in-thing for companies to label their products with catchwords and phrases that convey the sense of speed to the buyers.

The truth is, you are on your own if you pursue the realization of your destiny with the speed of a snail. God is a Person of speed, "...the LORD rideth upon a swift cloud" (Isaiah 19:1). The psalmist put it beautifully, "...runneth very swiftly..." (Ps. 147:15 The Word of God). The Spirit and the angels of God fly in their missions (Daniel 9:21). If you must go with God, you must make up your mind to be a person of speed.

I must inform you that speed is a requirement, a responsibility, and a risk. Life ends up in regrets if one gains speed without the capacity to manage it. In this book, you have 105 lessons on speed-virtues. Your life will never remain the same by the time you are through with it. You will both have speed and the ability to keep it. Your life is about to be revolutionized; you shall be turned to a fleet-footed person. You will overtake fast men as Elijah did (1 Kings 18:44-46).

Look at this,

The LORD God is my strength, and he will make my feet like hinds' feet, and he will make me to walk upon mine high places.

Hab. 3:19

You are about to encounter revelation for revolution. This is not a mere book; it is a manual to an extraordinary life. Do not read it like one of your novels. This is God's Word; and it has the capacity to turn a wanderer to a wonder to his generation. Get ready! God is about to set you in motion for speed unbeatable. God shall make you very, very fast. Beware! The best is about to happen to you.

CHAPTER ONE

COMMUNICATION SYSTEM

Communication is vital for speed. There is virtually nothing you do in this world that will not involve saying something. As far as you do something with people, you have to communicate. This is why most successful organizations have a department for communication manned by proficient speakers. In fact, some communication experts collect better remuneration than other more prestigious professionals.

If you know the right thing to say and how best to say it, you will never be slow in life. Some people are slow for being snared by their words. The Bible says, "Thou art snared with the words of thy mouth, thou art taken with the words of thy mouth. The wicked are trapped by their own words..." (Prov. 6:2; 12:13). Men of speed know what to say and how to say it to achieve desired speed.

You can be as rich as you desire. You can be as fast as you want. You only need to be more mindful of what you say and how you say it. The Bible says, "A man shall be satisfied with good by the fruit of his mouth...A man's belly shall be satisfied with the fruit of his mouth; and with the increase of his lips shall he be filled" (Prov. 12:14, 18:20). You can have the speed you desire if you give attention to the rules of good speech.

Many people are where they are today because they positively made use of the great power of communication. "Death and life are in the power of the tongue: and they that love it shall eat the fruit thereof" (Prov. 18:21). You can see that the Bible consistently speaks of "the fruit" of your mouth. There is so much good that can come to you if you can use your mouth properly.

In this system, we shall consider seven ways to say what you need to say appropriately. All over the world, people find it difficult to give expression to their intention—they have something good to say but end up saying it the wrong way. A Swahili Proverb said, "Better to stumble with the toe than with the tongue." A good food badly cooked does not make a good meal.

It is therefore how well you cook your words and serve them that make for speed. The following elements will impart positively on your manner of communication. You will sail fast for saying it well. You have power for speed in saying something and saying it very well.

RIGHTNESS

Your first responsibility in communication is to say what is right. Even if you season what is wrong with sweeteners, it is still wrong. What's right is what's best to be said. Wisdom says, "I will speak of excellent things; and the opening of my lips shall be right things" (Prov. 8:6). Men of wisdom and speed are known for speaking right things.

If you want speed, say right things. The truth is right at all times, just as a lie is wrong at all times. The right word is the truth and it prevails. The Bible says, "How forcible are right words!" (Job 6:25). The truth is strong—it does not need help to stand. But falsehood is paralyzed from birth—it needs permanent support. Right words, even the truth is universal—only lies are limited to the speakers.

Your concern should be how to speak words that are unequivocally right. Jesus Christ prayed, "Sanctify them through thy truth: thy word is truth" (John 17:17). The Word of God is the truth, even the right word. Whatsoever you say in accordance with God's Word is right. Right words please God and give speed.

The Bible says,

My son, if thine heart be wise, my heart shall rejoice, even mine. Yea, my reins shall rejoice, when thy lips speak right things.

Prov. 23:15-16

Also, whatever the Holy Spirit advises you to say is right—He is the Spirit of truth. Moses missed entering the Promised Land for his poor communication—he insulted God's people, "...ye rebels; must we fetch you water out of this rock?" (Num. 20:10). The Psalmist reported it this way, "They angered him also at the waters of strife, so that it went ill with Moses for their sakes: Because they provoked his spirit, so that he spake unadvisedly with his lips" (Ps. 106:32-33).

Look at this,

My covenant was with him of life and peace; and I gave them to him for the fear wherewith he feared me, and was afraid before my name. The law of truth was in his mouth, and iniquity was not found in his lips: he walked with me in peace and equity, and did turn many away from iniquity. For the priest's lips should keep knowledge, and they should seek the law at his mouth: for he is the messenger of the LORD of hosts.

Mal. 2:5-7

If you wait to be counselled by the Holy Spirit before you speak, you will speak right things. Insults, curses, threats and other forms of verbal violence are not right words. So, do not speak under provocation as the messenger of the LORD of hosts; because "...the wrath of man worketh not the righteousness of God" (James 1:20). Keep your words until your anger goes down.

Do not rush to say anything—give room for thoughtfulness. James the apostle counselled, "...my beloved brethren, let every man be swift to hear, slow to speak…" (James 1:19). Look at Today English Version of Psalms 106:33, "They made him so bitter that he spoke without stopping to think". Erasmus Darwin said, "…I have time to think before I speak…" Have time to stop to think before you speak—this is the way of the people of speed.

If you always speak before you stop to think, you will always have regrets for your speech and this is anti-speed. If you can just wait a minute, God will always give you "…the right words and such wisdom that none of your opponents will be able to reply! You will be given the right words at the right time" (Luke 21:15, Matt. 10:19). If you want speed, ever speak to be commended and never to be condemned.

Everyday God wants to give you right words as you pursue the realization of your destiny. The great man of speed requested, "Pray for me, too, and ask God to give me the right words as I boldly tell others about the Lord and as I explain to them that his salvation is for the Gentiles too" (Eph. 6:19 TLB). Your profession notwithstanding, God will give you right words that ensure speed.

If you talk thoughtlessly, your trip will be tough.

TIMELINESS

Timeliness is another indispensable element of the communication system of the speed systems. I went to speak to a Chief Executive Officer of a firm in favour of one of our church members. On getting there, I saw that the man was furious—he was seriously offended. God gave me right words but the time was not right. So, I greeted him and went back.

The Bible says,

There is a time for everything, a season for every activity under heaven.

Eccl. 3:1 NLT

You must know that there is the right time for the right words. If you say the right words at the wrong time, you will not get intended outcome. The Bible says, "A man hath joy by the answer of his mouth: and a word spoken in due season, how good is it! It is wonderful to say the right thing at the right time!" (Prov. 15:23).

New International Version says, "...how good is a timely word!" That God gives you the right words to say does not guarantee speed in life. Right words must be spoken at the right time to the right person at the right place to achieve the right results. That you have the right words does not make the circle of communication complete.

If you speak and you do not get a reply, you have not communicated effectively. It was Robert N. McMurry who said, "Chief executives repeatedly fail to recognize that for communication to be effective, it must be two-way." You encode while someone else decodes. To say the right words at the right time makes the receiver to respond well. Be watchful to know the right time for the right words.

Jesus Christ told His brethren,

My time is not yet come: but your time is always ready.

John 7:6

It is impossible to enjoy good speed if you cannot discern the right time to say what you need to say. In other words, speed will constantly elude you if you think you can say anything at anytime. You will be in trouble most times for what you say unmindful of the timing. The truth remains, "There is a right time for everything" (Eccl. 3:1 TLB). Always be sure that you say the right things at the right time. If the time is not ripe, hold your right words.

The Bible says, "How delightful is a timely word!" People need to delight in your words to respond positively to them. This is the reason you need to release the right words at the right time. If you must say a word, say "a timely word"

Timely speaking proves your maturity.

APTNESS

You may say the right words at the right time but do the words suit the situation? The suitability or the appropriateness of the truth you speak count in your speed-oriented communication. It is not enough that what you want to say is in agreement with God's Word; you are exhorted to speak "as fits the occasion" (Eph. 4:29 RSV).

Do not say the right words you ought to say on a comedy night in a funeral. The Bible says, "What a joy it is to find just the right word for the right occasion!" Let your communication be compatible with the circumstance. It was John Milton who said, "...apt words have power to cure the tumour of a troubled mind..." People are already in hell; help them with comforting words. God Himself speaks "kind and comforting words" (Zech. 1:13).

So, it is not only about what to say at the right time; it is also about saying what counts in that situation. See this, "The Lord GOD hath given me the tongue of the learned, that I should know how to speak a word in season to him that is weary: he wakeneth morning by morning, he wakeneth mine ear to hear as the learned" (Isaiah 50:4)

See another version,

The Sovereign LORD has taught me what to say, so that I can strengthen the weary.

Isaiah 50:4 TEV

Do not say what you ought to say to the merry to the weary. You must have appropriate words for each person you deal with.

This is how you communicate to encourage people and achieve speed. You cannot make the same speech for both a wedding and a funeral that will take place the same day in the same city. You would be wrong even if you were the Pope.

The Bible says,

A word fitly spoken is like apples of gold in pictures of silver. KJV

A word aptly spoken is like apples of gold in settings of silver. NIV

Like apples of gold in settings of silver is a word spoken in right circumstances. NASU

Prov. 25:11

Who will not like apples of gold in settings of silver? A word aptly spoken captures the essence of destiny – it proffers solution. A balm to festering wounds, a cold cup of water on a hot day, and a warm cup of tea on a cold morning: words are like these little acts that bring a bundle of joy to everyone. Do not give boiled water to people already in hell; if you do, they will curse you.

Show yourself a man of understanding in the affairs of others. Define yourself a man with "the tongue of the learned" by speaking appropriately to the weary and the merry. Jonathan Swift said, "Proper word in proper places make the true definition of style." God wants to teach you daily to speak aptly. This is a top secret for speed.

If you find a man with wounds, give him a balm.

SOFTNESS

Small men speak for applause but great men speak for impact. You need to speak to positively influence people for God. How you say your right words to achieve godly influence should be your top priority. Soft words are your strongest tools of influence.

They change people beyond your expectations. Do not be a man that throws words like stones at people whose lives are already fragile and possibly on the verge of wreckage. You will achieve no good result.

What John the Baptist could not achieve in Herod's life, Prophet Nathan achieved it with ease in the life of the greatest warrior of Israel. Consider his soft words, "There were two men in a certain town. One was rich, and one was poor. The rich man owned many sheep and cattle. The poor man owned nothing but a little lamb he had worked hard to buy. He raised that little lamb, and it grew up with his children. It ate from the man's own plate and drank from his cup. He cuddled it in his arms like a baby daughter.

One day a guest arrived at the home of the rich man. But instead of killing a lamb from his own flocks for food, he took the poor man's lamb and killed it and served it to his guest." David was furious. "As surely as the LORD lives," he vowed, "any man who would do such a thing deserves to die! He must repay four lambs to the poor man for the one he stole and for having no pity." Then Nathan said to David, "You are that man!" (2 Sam. 12:1-7 NLT).

There is no other way Prophet Nathan would have brought David to his knees than the way of soft, mild and gentle words. It looks weak but it is powerful. Never go to arrest a warrior with armour—go with tender words. It was with soft words that Jael, Heber's wife, arrested Sisera the great fighter. She said to him, "Turn in, my lord, turn in to me; fear not…" (Judges 4:18).

The Bible says,

A soft answer turneth away wrath: but grievous words stir up anger. KJV

A gentle answer quiets anger, but a harsh one stirs it up. TEV

Prov. 15:1

Diligently watch the men of speed, they are soft and gentle in words. No matter the profession, men with grievous and harsh words are slow. The choice is yours to make. Jacob prevailed over Esau's revengeful spirit with soft words. Abigail turned David from bloodshed with soft words. You can do much with soft words but very little with harsh words.

In the race of destiny, when you have a bone to break, never look for iron or stone. Ask God to give you soft words and you will succeed. The Bible says, "By long forbearing is a prince persuaded, and a soft tongue breaketh the bone...soft speech can crush strong opposition...a gentle tongue can break a bone" (Prov. 25:15). If you go softly, you can go through any man in the world.

Look at this,

The wrath of a king is as messengers of death, but a wise man will pacify it. AMP.

The anger of the king is a messenger of death, and a wise man will appease it. TLB

Prov. 16:14

How do you think a wise man pacifies or appeases the king's anger? It is by soft and gentle words. I have resolved crises many times using nothing but soft words. Make your decision today—change from grievous and harsh words to soft and gentle words. Repent from every form of verbal violence and you will experience indescribable speed. An Igede parable says, "It is with the softness of tongue that the earthworm lives with the ground."

Harshness is weakness, not strength.

SWEETNESS

A speed-oriented communication is not all about getting people to do what you want or taking advantage of their vulnerability. Your desire should be, "Anytime I speak, let people be tremendously blessed." Anywhere God sends His Word, people must receive blessings. God gives people what they need through His Word.

The Psalmist confessed,

The entrance of thy words giveth light; it giveth understanding unto the simple. He sent his word, and healed them, and delivered them from their destructions.

Ps. 119:130, 107:20

Your words should mean very significant things to people.

Thy word is a lamp unto my feet, and a light unto my path.

Ps. 119:105

As His Word does, trust God for your own words to meet people's needs. Your words can mean a great blessing to your world. It is sweet words that can add to people's lives and make them swift in life. Discouraging words subtract people's joy and deflate their passion for destiny realization. Brewster Higby, inspired by the beauty of Kansas, wrote a poem, "Oh give me a home...where seldom is heard a discouraging word". You will not have speed if you are a man loaded with poisonous words that destroy the peace and happiness of others. Sweet words leave the hearers blessed because they are mixed with godly virtues.

The Bible says,

Let your speech be always with grace, seasoned with salt, that ye may know how ye ought to answer every man.

Col. 4:6

Let no corrupt communication proceed out of your mouth, but that which is good to the use of edifying, that it may minister grace unto the hearers.

Eph. 4:29

Salt represents godly virtues in you. Jesus Christ exhorts that you should have salt in yourself (Mark 9:50). When your words are married to the goodness of the salt in you, they become sweet. You need to speak right words, even the truth. But you are exhorted to speak "the truth in love" (Col. 4:6). Love makes it sweet and helpful to the hearers. When you speak with grace, you distribute grace for uncommon progress. Gracious words impart grace to the hearers (Eph. 4:29).

You can ask the Lord to help you to always say words that are full of grace. It is possible to speak words that are gracious, pleasant and winsome at all times. Every word that is married to love, joy, peace, faith, hope, respect, humility, wisdom, patience, kindness, goodness, faithfulness, gentleness, self-control and anything called godly virtue must be sweet and helpful to your audience.

Consider Ephesians 4:29 from other versions of the Bible,

Don't use foul or abusive language. Let everything you say be good and helpful, so that your words will be an encouragement to those who hear them. NLT

Do not let any unwholesome talk come out of your mouths, but only what is helpful for building others up according to their needs, that it may benefit those who listen. NIV

Don't use bad language. Say only what is good and helpful to those you are talking to, and what will give them a blessing. TLB

Eph. 4:29

The time has come to speak with impact in view. The time has come to speak to release blessings to people. The time has come to speak and build others up in the areas of their needs. The time has come to speak and distribute benefits to your hearers. The time has come to speak and plant encouragement in the hearts of your people. The time has come to speak and raise the hope of your hearers.

Remember, words are like virgin maids waiting to be married to your inner virtues. Destiny realization happens swiftly when every word that comes out of your mouth is married to the virtues in you. It is therefore a strong opposition to your destiny to send out words without this holy solemnization. As each situation requires, let your words form a bond of consanguinity with love, humility, respect and all other godly virtues. Do you want to speak words seasoned with salt? Always ask yourself: What virtue can season this word?

Look at how the tenth leper seasoned his appreciation to Jesus Christ.

And one of them, when he saw that he was healed, turned back, and with a loud voice glorified God, And fell down on his face at his feet, giving him thanks: and he was a Samaritan.

Luke 17:15-16

To say thank you is the right word; but to fall down on his face at Jesus' feet made it the sweet word. It means the appreciation was done in humility. Any right word spoken along with relevant godly virtue must be sweet and will make for swiftness.

Take Patrick O'Keefe advice, "Say it with flowers".

SOUNDNESS

Apostle Paul, a man whose life personified speed, counselled his son in the faith, "Hold fast the form of sound words, which thou hast heard of me, in faith and love which is in Christ Jesus" (2 Tim. 1:13). He also told Titus to present "Sound speech, that cannot be condemned; that he that is of the contrary part may be ashamed, having no evil thing to say of you" (Titus 2:8).

Sound words are healthy words that do not contain venom and condemnation. One of the most crucial factors that determine the soundness of your words is that God is pleased. If your utterance carries divine seal of approval, no man can condemn you. Words that are nothing but a viper's venom attract heaven's displeasure and man's condemnation. Sound words are such that no friend or foe will "...be able to gainsay nor resist" (Luke 21:15).

Moses exited ministry with unsound words—God was displeased with him. He called Israel, "...ye rebels..." (Num. 20:10). See what God told him, "Because you did not trust me enough to

18

demonstrate my holiness to the people of Israel, you will not lead them into the land I am giving them!" (Num. 20:12 NLT). You see, sound words demonstrate God's holiness to people. This pleases God and aids destiny speed.

This is why when you speak soundly, people ask you of your God or your church. Sound words honour God but perverse words rubbish His Name before people. This is also why, as a child of God, when you speak unwholesome words, people ask whether you are still in the faith. People know the words that befit someone that professes faith in God.

You must therefore, on a daily basis, trust God enough to demonstrate His holiness to the people by speaking sound words. Speak to be ever commended and never condemned by God and man. Speak words that please God. Speak words that make people respect your God and you. Speak words that make your friends proud. Speak words that make your opponent feel ashamed because they have "no evil thing to say of you" (Titus 2:8).

God is no friend of evil speaking and you must trust Him never to let it come out of your mouth. The Bible is full of exhortation about this.

Let no corrupt communication proceed out of your mouth...Let evil speaking be put away from you...
Eph. 4:29, 31
Wherefore laying aside all malice, and all guile, and hypocrisies, and envies, and all evil speakings...
1 Peter 2:1
But now ye also put off all these; anger, wrath, malice, blasphemy, filthy communication out of your mouth.
Col. 3:8

Corrupt communication deepens the roots of moral decadence. The Bible says, "Be not deceived: evil communications corrupt good manners" (1 Cor. 15:33). This is one of the reasons the Psalmist prayed, "Let not an evil speaker be established in the earth...Let not a slanderer be established in the earth...Don't let liars prosper here in our land..." (Ps. 140:11). As diseases make a man sick, so do sin and wickedness perverse your words. Make the world a better place with your words.

Like Jesus Christ, you can live with no guile in your mouth.

For even hereunto were ye called: because Christ also suffered for us, leaving us an example, that ye should follow his steps; Who did no sin, neither was guile found in his mouth...

1 Peter 2:21-22

For he that will love life, and see good days, let him refrain his tongue from evil, and his lips that they speak no guile...

1 Peter 3:10

If you choose to speak corrupt words, do not forget what they attract—divine anger and punishment. Miriam spoke inappropriately against Moses because of his Ethiopian wife. She said, "Hath the LORD indeed spoken only by Moses? hath he not spoken also by us?" These words have the virus of disrespect, bitterness, envy, malice, hatred, etc. The surprising thing was that, the Bible says, "And the LORD heard it" (Num. 12:2). You need to be sober to speak because God hears all you say privately or publicly.

God was angry with Miriam because of her words. I believe you know what happened to her. "And the anger of the LORD was kindled against them; and he departed. And the cloud departed from off the tabernacle; and, behold, Miriam became leprous, white as snow: and Aaron looked upon Miriam, and, behold, she was leprous" (Num. 12:9-10). Do not speak to be judged by God; always speak to be blessed by Him.

The Lord Jesus Christ said,

But I say unto you, That...whosoever shall say to his brother, Raca, shall be in danger of the council: but whosoever shall say, Thou fool, shall be in danger of hell fire.

Matt. 5:22

You also remember how Ananias and Sapphira died in the house of God—they spoke words with falsehood deeply embedded (Acts 5:1-11).

Take this exhortation,
Be careful how you think; your life is shaped by your thoughts. Never say anything that isn't true. Have nothing to do with lies and misleading words.
Prov. 4:23-24 TEV

God asked Miriam, "...were ye not afraid to speak against my servant Moses?" It goes to mean that the fear of God is the root of sound words and the lack of it is the mother of rotten words. A criminal hurled insult at Jesus Christ and his fellow criminal asked him, "Don't you fear God?" (Luke 23:40 TEV). If you are God-fearing, you will always speak sound words.

The conclusion is that, "...by the fear of the LORD men depart from evil" (Prov. 16:6). By the fear of the LORD you can depart from every form of sinful words and be blessed for speed. It is so clear; if you do not mind your words, you cannot go far in the pursuit of your destiny.

Speak to be ever blessed and never punished.

FIRMNESS

There is so much to say about how to say what you need to say. Let your communication be with precision. Know well what you want to say and say it exactly, accurately and diligently. Always speak with every sense of earnestness. Let the person who hears you the first five minutes be willing to lend you his next forty minutes. This is the wisdom of great speakers.

You need to know when you made the point and when your audience got your point. Do not think you do well with many words. William Shakespeare said, "Men of few words are the best men". The Bible says, "As a dream comes when there are many cares, so the speech of a fool when there are many words...there is ruin in a flood of empty words" (Eccl. 5:3, 7). All your days, never be a man of many words. If you are not speaking to fools, say a word—for they say, "A word is enough for the wise".

A wise man said, "If you cannot say what you have to say in twenty minutes, you should go away and write a book about it." You see, you are in a generation that people do not have so much time to give to one thing. You must therefore know that, this is not a generation for parables. Nobody will come back to ask you what you mean. So, do not beat about the bush; hit the nail on the head.

Exercise high level of firmness with your words. You must mean every word you say. Have no idle word unless you are ready to account for it. Jesus Christ said, "That every idle word that men shall speak, they shall give account thereof in the day of judgment" (Matt. 12:36). Do not speak because you have a mouth—learn to speak because there is a very important need to do so.

The Bible says,

Suffer not thy mouth to cause thy flesh to sin; neither say thou before the angel, that it was an error: wherefore should God be angry at thy voice, and destroy the work of thine hands? KJV
Don't let your own words lead you into sin, so that you have to tell God's priest that you didn't mean it. Why make God angry with you? Why let him destroy what you have worked for? TEV

Eccl. 5:6

You need to know that inconsistency in your utterances is an invitation to God for the destruction of "the work of thine hands". You know what this means to your destiny speed. Do not invite God to destroy your business. You therefore need to be consistent with your words. Do not come back and tell your pastor "I did not mean what I said". God hates that kind of life. He wants you to say what you mean and mean what you say. Words are so spiritual and powerful—do not gamble with them.

You are exhorted not to be "double-tongued" (1 Tim. 3:8). Let nobody have any reason to doubt what you say. So, "...let your yea be yea; and your nay, nay..." (James 5:12). You need to be trusted to be entrusted with means of speed. Believe it, most times, you are trusted because you kept your words. So, live to be ever trusted—live true to your words.

Always stand by your words no matter the pressure. "And Pilate wrote a title, and put it on the cross. And the writing was, JESUS OF NAZARETH THE KING OF THE JEWS. Then said the chief priests of the Jews to Pilate, Write not, The King of the Jews; but that he said, I am King of the Jews. Pilate answered, What I have written I have written" (John 19:19-22).

Always stand by what you say, even when it hurts.

Who may worship in your sanctuary, LORD? Who may enter your presence on your holy hill? Those who...keep their promises even when it hurts. NLT
He always does what he promises, no matter how much it may cost. TEV

Ps. 15:1, 4

If you diligently think on the communication system of the speed systems, you will clearly see why some people are slow no matter how much they try. Your destiny speed will assume a higher dimension if you can improve on your manner of communication.

Let people believe your words
More than the sunrise and the sunset.

CHAPTER TWO

CONTACT SYSTEM

Grease and fluids are silent performers in your car. They may not make noise like the engine or run like the tyres but they do their work. They ensure harmony at every joint and prevent the failure of some principal elements. A car without grease will be too stiff for motion. Brake, clutch and others will fail without fluids.

In the pursuit of your vision, people are your greatest resource. Where there are no people, vision perishes. Men are God's means; they are His hands for the overflow of your bosom. Jesus Christ said, "Give, and it shall be given unto you; good measure, pressed down, and shaken together, and running over, shall men give into your bosom..." (Luke 6:38). You need grease and fluids to work smoothly and steadily with everyone you meet in the path of destiny.

Man to man relationship is as iron to iron contact. The meeting points cannot be smooth without grease. Disappointments and heartbreaks increase when relationships are greaseless. Grease is the reducer of friction and hostility. You need to know that hospitality, understanding, co-operation and support are products of greaseful relationships. No relationship can be graceful which is not first greaseful.

If the people that are in contact with you are not the assets of your vision, your life lacks the grease and the fluids for profitable relationship. This might be the reason you struggle and enjoy no speed in life. There is no speed for the man who does not know how to grease and oil his relationship with people. If you want speed, deliberately grease your contacts.

In the contact system of the speed systems, we will also consider seven elements that function as the grease and the fluids in your car. You shall be a better and a faster person, if you take God's counsel in this system. The potential people that have ever been around you will be turned to profitable people by the forces of grease and fluids.

You will always have a day to call others to be a part of your life.
> **And when they had this done, they inclosed a great multitude of fishes: and their net brake. And they beckoned unto their partners, which were in the other ship, that they should come and help them. And they came, and filled both the ships, so that they began to sink.**
> Luke 5:6-7

You are about to enjoy people as God intended that you should. You are about to uncover secrets that will bring to life your impaired relationships. Paul the apostle spoke to Timothy about Mark who he once rejected, "Take Mark, and bring him with thee: for he is profitable to me for the ministry" (2 Tim. 4:11). Have the following for your grease and fluids.

FRIENDLINESS

Friendliness greases every relationship. It is being a friend to others. You remember the words of Ralph W. Emerson, "The only way to have a friend is to be one." My definition of your friend is someone that multiplies your joy and subtracts your grief. Friendliness in your relationships means to say everything and do everything that multiply people's joy and minimize their sorrow.

There is no one you are friendly with that will not be an asset to you in one way or the other. And the more human assets you have, the higher your speed in life. God is our sole Source but we cannot deny His usage of men to advance our lives. Therefore, how we relate with men is completely important. I do not see how you will realize your vision if God does not use men to advance you.

The Bible says,

And the king Ahasuerus laid a tribute upon the land, and upon the isles of the sea. And all the acts of his power and of his might, and the declaration of the greatness of Mordecai, whereunto THE KING ADVANCED HIM...

Esther 10:1-2

You therefore have the responsibility to grease and oil your relationships. Be friendly with all your words and actions. To as many people as you can, multiply their joy and minimize their sorrow. Consider John Wesley's motto. "Do all the good you can, in all the ways you can, in all places you can, at all the times you can, to all the people you can, as long as ever you can."

Friendliness is the key to winning the hearts of men and this engenders speed in your life. If you carefully watch the attitude of men that struggle towards others, you will see unfriendliness and every form of hostility. You cannot repel people and enjoy speed in life. Do not multiply people's sorrow and minimize their joy and then expect to make progress yourself. God will always make happen to you what you make happen to others. And remember, the faster you want to go in life, the more people you need.

Proverbs 18:24 says, "A man that hath friends must shew himself friendly..." You must, not may, behave yourself friendly to have certain people around you. To relate with people with no sense of tenderliness and humour is to limit your own speed. To treat others with contempt does not show that you are superior to them; it only shows that you are a person of little wisdom.

How did Absalom steal the hearts of almost everyone in Israel? The Bible says, "And on this manner did Absalom to all Israel that came to the king for judgment: so Absalom stole the hearts of the men of Israel" (2 Sam. 15:6). Do you know the manner Absalom used to steal the hearts of the Israelites? It was the manner of friendliness.

Look at how He did it.

And it came to pass after this, that Absalom prepared him chariots and horses, and fifty men to run before him. And Absalom rose up early, and stood beside the way of the gate: and it was so, that when any man that had a controversy came to the king for judgment, then Absalom called unto him, and said, Of what city art thou? And he said, Thy servant is of one of the tribes of Israel.

And Absalom said unto him, See, thy matters are good and right; but there is no man deputed of the king to hear thee. Absalom said moreover, Oh that I were made judge in the land, that every man which hath any suit or cause might come unto me, and I would do him justice! And it was so, that when any man came nigh to him to do him obeisance, he put forth his hand, and took him, and kissed him.

2 Sam. 15:1-5

As you can see, the manner was of friendliness. To Absalom, it was all about rising on time, meeting people and showing care for their concerns. It was all about giving them hope in life. It was all about giving people the right feeling; to let them know that they were not mere slaves meant to labour for the king but worthy and cherished people, good enough to be kissed. You need to understand that everyone wants to be loved.

Remember the words of Ruth to Boaz,
Let me find favour in thy sight, my lord; for that thou hast comforted me, and for that thou hast spoken friendly unto thine handmaid, though I be not like unto one of thine handmaidens.
Ruth 2:13

I do not think it is a sin to steal people's hearts and lead them to the center of the will of God for their lives. You can completely steal any heart by friendliness. If Absalom had a good purpose and God's backing, even David would not have withstood him with what the force of friendliness did for him. By friendliness, he mobilized almost the entire nation behind himself. With God, achieving anything would have been a walkover.

With your good vision from God, you can get many people to help you by emulating this manner of friendliness. If you are friendly with people in your words and actions, you can win anybody. Proverbs 22:11 says, "He that loveth pureness of heart, for the grace of his lips the king shall be his friend." Do you know what it means for the Governor of your State to be your loyal friend? Without pretense, it means speed in life.

Like the irons in the different parts of your car, some people are too hard to deal with. Your instrument of influence over them is the grease of friendliness. A woman met a herbalist and complained about the hostility of her husband and requested for a love-charm. The herbalist promised to help her if she could get the hair of a living lion for the preparation of the spell.

The woman declined but the herbalist convinced her and sent her to the forest where only one young lion stayed. The instruction was for her to give the lion a kid-goat for three days at the same time. The woman went with the goat the first day and as the lion came in its fierceness, she dropped it and left. The second day, the lion's fierceness came down drastically.

On the third day, as the lion sighted the woman it wagged its tail. This made the woman know that the lion won't hurt her. She went very close and dropped the kid before it and pulled out its hair. She excitedly went to the herbalist for the magic-charm, only for the herbalist to say, "Go and be friendly with your husband as you were with the lion."

By friendliness, you can make the lion a part of your vision and be sure you can catch anything that requires might. How friendly are you? There is no gain whatsoever in hurting people's hearts. People are already facing trying moments and their healing awaits your friendliness. You can help so many people if only you are friendly.

You can also win back any destiny helper you lost to misunderstanding. Only gird yourself with friendliness. The Bible says, "And her husband arose, and went after her, to speak friendly unto her, and to bring her again..." (Judges 19:1-3). As far as human beings are concerned, you will control them if only you are friendly

There is no length people will not go with you, if you deliberately make them feel loved. This is what the grease of friendliness does for you. Let the next person you meet know you have really changed and you will see drastic change in your destiny speed.

"There is a friend that sticketh closer than a brother".

IDENTIFICATION

Another very important element of the contact system is identification. It makes your relationship functional and profitable. Mother Teresa, in her time said, "The biggest disease today is not leprosy and tuberculosis but rather the feeling of being unwanted". Everyone in a relationship with you have this feeling. It is only your warm identification that kills it.

Two of our church members almost lost a very profitable relationship. They felt it was of no serious significance to attend the burial of the man's daughter. When the burial was over and the man returned to town, offence had taken over the place of his affection for them. If they had made efforts and attended the burial, they would have greased and oiled that relationship.

It is for the sake of identification that the Bible exhorts us to "Rejoice with them that do rejoice, and weep with them that weep" (Rom. 12:15). You cannot be a man of speed, if you stay aloof when others are happy or sad. You see, the men you need for speed need your cheers in their times of joy and your comfort in their times of grief.

Why was God unhappy with the Ammonites and Moabites? They failed to identify with the Israelites when it mattered most.

The LORD said,

An Ammonite or Moabite shall not enter into the congregation of the LORD; even to their tenth generation shall they not enter into the congregation of the LORD for ever: Because they met you not with bread and with water in the way, when ye came forth out of Egypt...

Deut. 23:3-4

There are moments in people's lives that you need to meet them with bread and water. They need them to praise God and shake off the ill-feeling of not being loved and wanted. I have seen people cried on their wedding day for one reason: the people they expected did not show up. Denial of identification can be very painful to your well-wishers and of no gain to you. So, learn to identify with your loved ones in every way you can.

Consider these last words of David; they were his orders to Solomon on how to deal with those that positively identified with him in his trying moments and those that added salt to his injuries.

But shew kindness unto the sons of Barzillai the Gileadite, and let them be of those that eat at thy table: for so they came to me when I fled because of Absalom thy brother.

And, behold, thou hast with thee Shimei the son of Gera, a Benjamite of Bahurim, which cursed me with a grievous curse in the day when I went to Mahanaim: but he came down to meet me at Jordan,

and I sware to him by the LORD, saying, I will not put thee to death with the sword.

Now therefore hold him not guiltless: for thou art a wise man, and knowest what thou oughtest to do unto him; but his hoar head bring thou down to the grave with blood.

1 Kings 2:7-9

You can see how God and man respond to genuine identification. God said, "...Because they met you not with bread and with water in the way, when ye came forth out of Egypt..." David said, "...for so they came to me when I fled because of Absalom thy brother." There are people you need to meet with, speak with, give to and stay with when certain things happen whether gladness or grief.

This is one way to grease and oil your contacts for profitable relationship. Check the man whose bosom is always empty; he does not know how to grease and oil the men God uses to bless his own bosom. To be spiritually high and socially low is to be slow in life. If you want to be a man and a woman of speed, have this manner; show up positively in the affairs of others.

Many men of means attend four to five occasions in a weekend. They identify, grease and oil the contacts they need. The truth is, you will one day need those you identify with. Those you go to hail or help could be instrumental to your speed in life. Learn to be a part of people's lives and situations.

Remember Joseph: he shared the grief of the Butler and gave him hope. In due time, the same butler spoke well of him before the king and that led to his elevation to the office of the Prime Minister. Mordecai would not have had any relevance if he had not raised and pushed Esther to her place in destiny. The ways of God are truly mysterious; the little girl grew and became the bridge to her uncle's prominence.

Look at this,

And Mordecai came before the king; for Esther had told what he was unto her. And the king took off his ring, which he had taken from Haman, and gave it

unto Mordecai. And Esther set Mordecai over the house of Haman.

Esther 8:1-2

John Cassis said, "Nobody cares how much you know until they know how much you care." Genuine identification shows everyone around you that you really care. God blesses this and men reciprocate it. This is your way to high speed. Let your heart be filled with compassion; pick that helpless Esther and train her. Open your eyes and see that Butler with grief on his face and interpret his dream.

You may not bring Lazarus out of the grave, but you can go and comfort Mary and Martha. Be sensitive in the spirit to know when someone is broken-hearted and sorrowful; identify with them and proffer your support. Encourage that David with that wayward Absalom. Carry some bread and water for that weary family in the wilderness of life.

Be full of kindness and goodness; show yourself merciful in the affairs of others. Make everyone around you feel indebted to you. Make many people to ever look for good opportunities to reciprocate your kindness and goodwill to them. If you lack speed, check your men. If you lack men, check your genuine and positive identification with people.

You crash my back, I crash your back
Isn't a bad cliché after all.

THANKSGIVING

Look at this story from Luke 17:11-19; As Jesus continued on toward Jerusalem, he reached the border between Galilee and Samaria. As he entered a village there, ten lepers stood at a distance, crying out, "Jesus, Master, have mercy on us!" He looked at them and said, "Go show yourselves to the priests." And as they went, their leprosy disappeared.

One of them, when he saw that he was healed, came back to Jesus, shouting, "Praise God, I'm healed!" He fell face down on the ground at Jesus' feet, thanking him for what he had done. This man was a Samaritan. Jesus asked, "Didn't I heal ten men? Where are the other nine? Does only this foreigner return to give glory to God?" And Jesus said to the man, "Stand up and go. Your faith has made you well."

Thanksgiving is another strong element of the contact system. In your relationship with people, they identify with you in one way or the other. Do not think your goodness is the reason for people's kindness to you. This thinking pattern kills the spirit of gratitude in you and you exist as an ungrateful and thankless person.

See people's identification with you coming from their own goodness. Jacob told God, "I am not worthy of the least of all the mercies, and of all the truth, which thou hast shewed unto thy servant…" (Gen. 32:10). See yourself therefore as a debtor to thank everyone that stretches forth a hand of kindness to you. You must grease and oil your relationships with thanksgiving.

You grease your relationships to make them more functional and profitable. This is the excellent work thanksgiving knows how best to do. The Samaritan in our text above got a better relationship and a better blessing with thanksgiving. If you see a man who cannot say thank you to the people who genuinely stand with him, avoid him. He will not go far in life. The man who mistakenly helped him the first time, will not help him the second time.

If you know how to appreciate people again and again, you will enjoy their positive identification again and again. Any kindness you cannot exchange thanks for, do not receive it. But if you receive a needle-kindness, you are indebted to give thanks. Always give thanks and give it promptly. To me, it is completely inappropriate not to reciprocate kindness with thanks within 24 hours of reception. The tenth leper returned to give glory to God just as he saw that he was healed.

Be lavish with your thanks. To me, it is also unseemly to give thanks only once for any kindness received. Give thanks until the receiver feels indebted to thank you for thanking him. Give thanks until the receiver does a new thing for you. Give thanks again and again. The repetition of thanks is the real proof of gratitude. And remember, there is no too much to giving of thanks.

An ethnic group in Nigeria has a good spirit of gratitude. When you show them kindness, they will reverentially thank you immediately. When they see you the next day, they will say, "thank you for yesterday." When they meet you two days later, they will say, "thank you for the day before yesterday." When they meet you after three days, they will say, "thank you for that day." They continue in this circle from one kindness to another.

This is how to grease and oil your relationships. Never be known as an ungrateful and thankless person. You will have rough times dealing with people the second time if you are not a thanksgiver. Whether you know it or not, God and men are happy when you give thanks because they identify with you. If you lack men for speed, check your level of thankfulness.

Poor attitude of gratitude will deny you great blessings. You need to deliberately pray like George Hubert: "Thou O LORD hast given so much to me, give me one more thing - a grateful heart." You need a grateful heart that flows with appreciation towards God and the people He uses to bless you. If you are too big to appreciate, you are too small to accelerate in life.

If your tanks are empty, check your thanks.

GIFTS-GIVING

The best way to substantiate your thanksgiving is to accompany it with gifts. If you are really grateful, strengthen your thanks with gifts, whether big or small. Relationships need to be serviced. Giving of gifts is one of the most powerful ways to service a relationship. Nothing proves your love in a relationship as gifts-giving and it greatly greases and oils your contacts.

> **For God so loved the world, that he gave his only begotten Son, that whosoever believeth in him should not perish, but have everlasting life. Greater love hath no man than this, that a man lay down his life for his friends.**
>
> John 3:16, 15:13

Do not tell people you love them when for years you cannot afford the smallest gift. It is better you let your gifts speak than to pour empty words of love. God's love is proven to us by the release of His son to us. You cannot continue to relate with people and they cannot point at anything you have released to grease their relationship with you.

Gifts have their mysterious ways into the hearts of people. A little gift can make the king your friend. Do not think anybody is so small or great to resist the force of your gifts. Give gifts to everyone in a relationship with you. Take a gift to your president as his gardener. Never say he will not need it. Give a gift to that gatekeeper and never mind what he thinks. You give your gifts and leave the rest to God.

Do you know what will happen in your life? God will multiply back to you the gifts you give. "Give, and it shall be given unto you; good measure, pressed down, and shaken together, and running over, shall men give into your bosom. For with the same measure that ye mete withal it shall be measured to you again" (Luke 6:38).

People shall overwhelmingly like you. The Bible says, "Many will intreat the favour of the prince: and every man is a friend to him that giveth gifts" (Prov. 19:6). If you want to gather many people for your vision, be the man that gives gifts. If you do not know how to get friends and keep them, please try the way of gifts-giving. You will have "every man" coming for you.

Your gifts will create opportunities for you and bring you new contacts. I see that those I give gifts introduce me to people higher than they are. This is to prove what the Bible says, "A man's gift maketh room for him, and bringeth him before great men" (Prov. 18:16). I used to find it difficult to understand why I am too favourably disposed to people that give me gifts. I thought I was greedy and needed to change but it was not greed.

I also discovered that every receiver of my gifts, including very senior men in the ministry, are also favourably disposed to me. I came to understand Proverbs 19:6, that, "every man", excluding nobody, is favourably disposed to him that giveth gifts. Every man with no exception can be on your side as a giver of gifts. This is the disposition of others you need for speed in life.

Someone was surprised at the crowd in one of my book presentations. He knew that people are always scanty in a book launch but surprised that people were scouting for seats, including the representative of my State Governor. You see, I have what I call advance love-commitment. I love people when I do not need them to do anything for me. I identify with people and give them gifts when I do not need their help. I never wait to have a need or a programme before I remember people in relationship with me. So, many people wait to return my kindness and warmth. They wait for an opportunity to identify with me before one comes. You are too small if you go to people only when you are in dire need.

Do you still remember the story of the woman that made lion her friend? Your gifts-giving works wonders, even with animals, whether they are in the house or in the bush. It is not anybody's fault; it is rather God's eternal order for everyone and everything to respond positively to goodwill and kindness that gifts represent. Even the trees bend their necks to where the rays of the sun are. Consider that story again and see that you need to give gifts again and again to win more helpers of destiny speed.

A woman met a herbalist and complained about the hostility of her husband and requested for a love-charm. The herbalist promised to help her if she could get the hair of a living lion for the preparation of the spell. The woman declined but the herbalist convinced her and sent her to the forest where only one young lion stayed. The instruction was for her to give the lion a kid-goat for three days at the same time. The woman went with the goat the first day and as the lion came in its fierceness, she dropped it and left. The second day, the lion's fierceness came down drastically. On the third day, as the lion sighted the woman it wagged its tail.

The first time was introduction; the second time was consolidation and the third time was victory. Never be a man that congratulates yourself after an attempt. What you need for speed is victory in your efforts, not attempt. So, keep on the attempts until you win. No man is too cheap, so, do not be casual in your approach to have them as your destiny helpers. Jacob had no other way to greet Esau his aggrieved brother. It was best to grease him with a gift.

"You must say, 'Yes, your servant Jacob is right behind us.' "Jacob was thinking, "I will win him over with the gifts, and when I meet him, perhaps he will forgive me." He sent the gifts on ahead of him and spent that night in camp" (Gen. 32:20-21 TEV). If you are stingy, you cannot win in the battle of life.

Jacob sent intimidating gifts.

After spending the night there, Jacob chose from his livestock as a present for his brother Esau: 200 female goats and 20 males, 200 female sheep and 20 males, 30 milk camels with their young, 40 cows and 10 bulls, 20 female donkeys and 10 males.

Gen. 32:13 TEV

Gifts-giving means living to be assisted by "every man". To live otherwise is to live to be resisted. I have seen men who prepared themselves to resist me change their minds by the power of a little gift. I did not know their plans before I gave them gifts but their confessions revealed their ill-intentions. But thank God for the prosperity of the gift-mission.

The Bible says,

A gift is as a precious stone in the eyes of him that hath it: whithersoever it turneth, it prospereth.

Prov. 17:8

You can send a gift on a mission to all those relationships that are cold, non-functioning and fruitless. There is always prosperity in the gift-mission. Those relationships will be revivified and revitalized and this is one vital fulcrum of speed. Never keep your contact points greaseless. Send a gift on a greasing mission and it will prosper. If you lack supporters of speed, check your gift-mission field, it must be very dry.

When last did you send out a gift?

APPEAL

An experienced man said, "a please is stronger than a kiss." People value your appeal more than your power. A fearful man can obey you because of your power but what will the powerful man obey you for. The only instrument that can make the fearful and the powerful to function profitably towards you is appeal.

Do not try to lord it over anybody; it is not God's way. "Jesus told them, "In this world the kings and great men order their slaves around, and the slaves have no choice but to like it! But among you, the one who serves you best will be your leader. Out in the world the master sits at the table and is served by his servants. But not here! For I am your servant" (Luke 22:25-27 TLB).

If you must work with others in harmony, the fluid of appeal must be a daily part of your communication. Do not send anybody (including your biological children) you are not ready to offer the gentle word "PLEASE". As you drive on the road, you will find at the back of long vehicles an inscription, "Horn before overtaking". In your destiny journey, say please before you take advantage. You will achieve more if you stop taking others for granted.

Say, please, get me some water. Please, get all the tables here. Please, go and receive the guests. Please, clear the table when the guests are through. Please, change the bulbs in the runway. Please, wash the car very early tomorrow. Please, follow me to the market today. Please, dispatch the letters before the close of work. Please, send the mail to all the partners at noon.

It is relationship-greasing to start your instructions with a word or words of appeal. You may choose to end with please but I would prefer you start with it. It is needless to horn after you have overtaken. The age and the status of the person you deal with notwithstanding, make appeals and avoid commands. To say please does not reduce your personality and authority. It only reveals you a man who knows the science of relating with other self-conscious beings.

Do not give people the impression that you want to use your power on them. They will never assist you; they will rather resist you to a stand still. Do not let people obey or do things for you under duress. Make your appeals and allow people to respond willingly and out of their own pleasure. Your aides of speed cannot come out of people you intimidate.

Even the Lord Jesus Christ speaks in this manner,

"Come to me, all of you who are tired from carrying heavy loads, and I will give you rest. Take my yoke and put it on you, and learn from me, because I am gentle and humble in spirit; and you will find rest. For the yoke I will give you is easy, and the load I will put on you is light."

Listen! I stand at the door and knock; if anyone hears my voice and opens the door, I will come into his house and eat with him, and he will eat with me.

Matt. 11:28-30, Rev. 3:20-21 TEV

The Lord Jesus never came with commands but appeals. He never in any place told us to obey Him. He encourages us to do His Word. You obey commanders; but you follow leaders and do what their lives and words say. We follow Jesus in doing what Himself both did and taught. If the Lord himself used appeals with humanity and captured the whole world, you may need to reconsider your manner of conversation. Coercion is not strength but deficiency in character.

Paul the apostle was a man of tremendous speed and you remember that his epistles were full of "I beseech you". You know what that means? It means, "I plead with you". You will find other synonyms for beseech and they all convey appeal. As the planter of most of the early churches, Paul could have decided to lord it over them but he did not. He used appeals with his followers like no other writer of the Bible.

Look at this,

As apostles of Christ we certainly had a right to make some demands of you, but we were as gentle among you as a mother feeding and caring for her own children. We loved you so much that we gave you not only God's Good News but our own lives, too.

1 Thess. 2:7-8 NLT

Paul's disposition to compassionate appeal does not portray him a weak man. Rather, it showed his strength of character and authority, his ability to moblise people with little effort, and his good understanding on how to work with others. Pride is a weakness of character and the very reason some men will never say please to others.

Many people wonder why I control people very easily. I build my power and authority into love, good understanding and irresistible appeals. I always refuse to force my way through; I rather grease my way through with people. In our ministry, I rule nobody and I lord it over no one. I love to lead people in Christ's kind of life. I have trained myself to say please before I overtake. I say to the least person in my house, "Please, get me" this or that.

To respect people's rights and to appeal to their kind hearts is more profitable than to use threats, intimidation and coercive force. Mildness only appears weak but it is the strongest rope to draw people into your vision. Have you ever considered this Scripture, "Blessed are the meek: for they shall inherit the earth"

(Matt. 5:5). The earth is not for people who use coercive force to make others act against their will.

You do not need to roar like a lion to show you are powerful. A person of authority does not shout or flex his muscles to make people fall in line. He uses the force of meekness to make others come along. Your words can be gods over people if you are a man with strong appeals. Abigail only had the weapon of appeal but she turned David and his warriors back.

Look at this,

For I am a man under authority, having soldiers under me: and I say to this man, Go, and he goeth; and to another, Come, and he cometh; and to my servant, Do this, and he doeth it.

Matt. 8:9

If you are a man of strong appeals, you will achieve more than an Army General. You will say to this man, please go and he will go with pleasure. You will say to another person, please come and he will come out of his own pleasure. You will say to your servant, please do this and he will do it with all happiness. You must know that people hate to be compelled, especially by coercion. Use appeals.

Consider the manner of conversation in our ministry, "James, please come. Yes sir. How are you? I'm fine, sir. I would like to send you somewhere. Okay sir. Please, get bottled water across the road for me. Okay sir. Thank you, my dear. It is my pleasure, sir". James was not bullied. He was called with an appeal. He was asked after his well-being. He was given the chance to decline the errand. He was sent with an appeal. He was thanked for his willingness.

Never ask: Why do I pay him? You must learn to respect people and their rights. Make people do things by pleasure and not under pressure. You are lubricating your relationships for functionality and profitability if you speak with the tone of appeal than authority. Never be the lion everyone fears; instead, be the man everyone loves to work with.

I would like to implore you to change your rough manner of communication and adopt the way men of speed converse with people. If please is absent from their sentences, then modal verbs (would, could, should) must be present. The Bible says, "Buy the truth, and sell it not; also wisdom, and instruction, and understanding" (Prov. 23:23). You can surround yourself with helpers of speed if your mouth can learn the golden word "PLEASE".

You can grease your way through with anybody.

COMPLIMENT

Compliment is another strong element in the contact system of the speed systems. Compliment is a heartfelt expression of your impression. In other words, it is a way of expressing your appreciation for the qualities you see in a person. This is another vital element that makes you go places. It was Abraham Lincoln who said, "Everybody likes a compliment." If everybody likes a compliment, you can win everybody with it.

Compliment is the child of your proper vision of people. You need to see people well, note their sterling uniqueness, get impressed with it and express it with sincerity and warmth. There are people that see nothing good in others. You cannot be impressed by what you do not see and you cannot warmly express what does not impress you.

The truth is, you do not see people as they are; you rather see them as you are. To a bad man, everybody is bad and he has an insult for them all. To a good man, everybody is good in one way or the other and he has a compliment for them. In the pursuit of your destiny, you must ask God for the good eye that sees people as He does.

Your vision of people, your impression with their goodness and your expression of it go together. There is no way you "see men as trees" that you can ever be impressed about anything in them (Mark 8:24). Most people just need the Lord's second touch in their vision of people. "After that he put his hands again upon his eyes, and made him look up: and he was restored, and saw every man clearly" (Mark 8:25).

When you see "every man clearly", even as they are in God's own eyes, your mouth will be full of compliments for people. You still remember that man was created in the image and likeness of God.

And God said,

Let us make man in our image, after our likeness: and let them have dominion over the fish of the sea, and over the fowl of the air, and over the cattle, and over all the earth, and over every creeping thing that creepeth upon the earth. So God created man in his own image, in the image of God created he him; male and female created he them.

Gen. 1:26-27

By the fall of man, he was short of God's glory but not devoid of it. So that, no matter how depraved a man might be, there is an element of God's goodness left behind in him in one area or the other. There is therefore no man that is totally unworthy of a compliment.

Look at this,

By faith the harlot Rahab perished not with them that believed not, when she had received the spies with peace.

Heb. 11:31

What do you say to a harlot that genuinely likes pastors? It is just for you to fix the eye of God and search for that good and unique thing that can buy your compliment for people. I always have one thing that impresses me about everyone and I keep my compliments on it.

Do not be a man that is dedicated to find people's faults and to tell them to their faces. It means everybody will hate you and that is unprofitable to your destiny pursuit. People who see too many flaws in others have so many insults; but men of speed see so much good in others and they have a good word for everyone. You can choose to be either full of insults or compliments.

You gain nothing with insults but compliments are your grease and fluid for speed. Do not take for granted anything everyone appreciates. When you give people what they like, you naturally become who they like. But when you give people what they hate, you also naturally become who they hate. Everyone likes a compliment—just give it to each person you meet.

You see, people already know their values, virtues, graces, efforts and achievements. A compliment is simply to remind people of the good they already know they have. Dr. George Akume, former Governor of Benue State reminded me of the obvious with his compliment, "You are such a wonderful writer". He said many things as a Governor, but this I will not forget.

The truth is, you need people to like you and stand with you in life. Do that wonderful thing they all like—give them compliments in every way you can. Say words to place value on their goodness and specialty. Give commendations that make others see them in a positive light. Send a gift and tell them you covet their great graces. Do souvenirs that herald their outstanding performances.

If you cannot do so much, at least, say a good word. It costs you nothing to say something good and truthful about someone. The woman of Tekoah said unto King David,

My lord is wise, according to the wisdom of an angel of God, to know all things that are in the earth.

2 Sam. 14:20

Abigail also commended him,

For the LORD will certainly make my lord a sure house; because my lord fighteth the battles of the LORD, and evil hath not been found in thee all thy days.

1 Sam. 25:28

If you can go beyond a word of warmth, then give rewards to encourage people in those areas they have consistently done well. Give titles, conferment, awards and certificates of excellence in the areas they have contributed significantly. Send cards and letters of appreciation and congratulations. Organize receptions, thanksgiving services and parties in their honour. There is nothing you do that will be too much to give a heartfelt compliment to someone of worth.

The queen of Sheba gave king Solomon "$3,500,000 in gold, along with a huge quantity of spices and precious gems" as a compliment for his wisdom (1 Kings 10:10 TLB). There are so many things to say and do to let people know you appreciate God's grace and glory in their lives. In its purposes and functions, compliment is akin to grease; and you need it to keep your relationships on an even keel. It works wonders in the pursuit of destiny.

People appreciate you when they know you appreciate them too. People support your progress when they know you are in love with theirs. You have nothing to gain if people perceive you as an enemy of progress. By your compliments, let people know that you support their advancement. This is your own secret for unovertakable speed.

Mind you, this wisdom is not intended to make you a sycophant, a flatterer and a cheap praise-singer of haters of God who have impoverished their communities. The Bible says, "A lying tongue hates its victims, and flattery causes ruin" (Prov. 26:28 NLT). A genuine compliment is safe but flattery is destructive. So, do not say a word of warmth that is not the reality.

The prophets of Jerusalem...encourage and compliment those who are doing evil instead of turning them back from their sins. These prophets are as thoroughly depraved as the men of Sodom and Gomorrah were.

Jer. 23:14 TLB

Your compliments should not be borne out of your greed for the things in people's hands. Your compliments should be your most sincere and warmest expression for the grace and glory of God you see in people. The Bible says, "In the end, people appreciate frankness more than flattery" (Prov 28:23 NLT). So, never give the compliment of a fool.

It is better to be criticized by a wise man than to be praised by a fool! For a fool's compliment is as

quickly gone as paper in fire, and it is silly to be impressed by it.
Eccl. 7:5-6 TLB

Make your compliments in such a way that God can borrow your words and deeds of appreciation for the same person.

Take a census of your supporters,
99.9% of them will be those you gave compliments.

APOLOGY

You are a genuine man but not a perfect one. No matter how carefully you conduct yourself, offences find their ways into your very functional and profitable relationship. Jesus Christ said, "It is impossible but that offences will come" (Luke 17:1). To many people, relationship ends where offence intrudes. You need to know that offences are intruders and they should be shown the way out of your relationships.

Sincere apology is the weapon against offence-intruders. It only costs you your pride to sincerely say, "I am very sorry for what I have done" and have your relationship back again. So many people have destroyed relationships meant for their lifting only for an insignificant offence. Do not sacrifice any relationship on the altar of grievances.

So, be quick to sincerely apologise and be ever willing to receive it and let relationship continue. If your mistakes do not end, never let your apology end. And you must also realize that people are human; they continue to make mistakes. Be as your Father in heaven and forgive them as many times they sincerely express regrets for their wrong deeds towards you.

Jesus Christ said,
Even if he wrongs you seven times a day and each time turns again and asks forgiveness, forgive him.
Luke 17:4 NLT

"Then Peter came to him and asked, Lord, how often should I forgive someone who sins against me? Seven times? No! Jesus replied, seventy times seven!" (Matt. 18:21 NLT). God does not want to turn you to a person that keeps records of offence. No! He only wants you to realize that someone can err and also apologize again and again; and that the offended should find a place in his heart to forgive as many times he is entreated.

If you take apology and forgiveness away from any relationship, the remains will be an insignificant fragment and that cannot aid speed. You therefore need to make use of the grease of apology and forgiveness. Humble yourself and apologise; but when it is the other way round, be merciful and forgive. Place value on your relationship and do not just easily exchange it for an offence. Will you cut your head because you find lice in your hair?

Cast out your pride and always learn to say "I am very sorry for my misdemeanour". Apology is not only for the older people you offend. It is for everyone you offend, including people younger and junior to you. If you do not want to apologise to your younger ones and junior staff, do not offend them. If you cannot stop because you are human, never stop to apologize to them. You may not know it now but the little Esther of today might be your access to the people that matter to your destiny tomorrow. Gifts grease relationship quiet well but they are not substitutes for apology. Do not give a gift to someone you first need to give apology. All you need is to humble yourself, open your mouth and express regrets for your misdeed. There are people that will feel insulted if you give them gifts when you ought to have said you are sorry for your wrong doing. Leave that gift and go to apologize with deep remorse and repentance.

The Psalmist said,

I am deeply sorry for what I have done.

Ps. 38:18 NLT

Do not try to justify yourself before you end up with "I am sorry for what I did". There is no good reason to hurt anyone and therefore explanations are totally irrelevant here. All you need to do is to apologize and regain the relationship. But do not merely say "Sorry", "Sorry sir" or "I am sorry" to someone you have offended; that is inappropriate. These are not the right words of apology. An enlightened person will be more offended that you say "Sorry sir". Are you expressing pity because he is bereaved or depraved in character? Do not let anyone misunderstand your apology.

True apology involves your person, your regrets and your mention of the wrong. "I am" represents you, "deeply sorry" your regrets and "for what I have done" the wrong. If you really want to apologise, then, put the three parts together. Like the Psalmist, always say, "I am deeply sorry for what I have done." This I believe will attract the mercy and the forgiveness of the offended.

You need to know that the devil has no business with unprofitable relationships. He comes to destroy relationships meant for the realization of destiny. You must therefore never give place to the devil through offences. You remember the relationship of Jesus Christ and John the Baptist. This was a spiritual, destiny-based relationship and the devil threw an offence into it.

Learn something from the Lord's reply to John the Baptist,

Go and shew John again those things which ye do hear and see: The blind receive their sight, and the lame walk, the lepers are cleansed, and the deaf hear, the dead are raised up, and the poor have the gospel preached to them. And blessed is he, whosoever shall not be offended in me.

Matt. 11:4-6

Do not be a man that goes about only to pick offences here and there. You must ignore the offences the devil throws into your relationship. This will tremendously give speed to the realization of your destiny. But, if you have given yourself to the devil as an instrument of offence, you must know that there is no gain whatsoever in offending people here and there. "It is impossible but that offences will come: but woe unto him, through whom they come!" (Luke 17:1).

Of a truth, God is interested in your reconciliation with people. Hear this, "So if you are standing before the altar in the Temple, offering a sacrifice to God, and suddenly remember that a friend has something against you, leave your sacrifice there beside the altar and go and apologize and be reconciled to him, and then come and offer your sacrifice to God" (Matt. 5:23-24 TLB

If you want to be a man of speed, learn to say "I am sorry for what I did" in the once-in-a-while times you err as human. As simple as it is, it will do you a lot of good. Is there someone you need to go to right now and sincerely say, "I am so sorry for what I said?" You do not need to delay. This is the time to get up and go to say those words that dissolve offence and restore relationships.

The prodigal son said,

I will get up and go to my father and say, Father, I have sinned against God and against you. I am no longer fit to be called your son; treat me as one of your hired workers. So he got up and started back to his father.

Luke 15:18-20 TEV

All that you have learned in this chapter is to enhance your relationship with people so that your vision will not perish. For where there are no people, vision perishes.

Men are God's hands for the fullness and the overflow
Of your bosom—deal wisely with them.

CHAPTER THREE

SECURITY SYSTEM

Know this today, of all of God's creation on earth, only the devil and the fallen angels operate without divine purpose. They were not sent to the earth by God like you and I. They have no divine assignment on earth. They meet no need, solve no problem or answer any question on behalf of God.

The devil is on his own on earth. His goals to steal, kill and destroy are self-imposed. He has nobody to report to at the end of time. He is only waiting for God's final judgment. So, the greatest thing the devil hates is destiny. He attacks people's destinies right from the womb. He killed some great children even before they were born.

He raged through Herod—he wanted to kill the King of the Jews within the month of his birth. Thank God he did not succeed, even as he has not succeeded in terminating your life, and he will never succeed. Satan hates you because he can never be like you. You are destined for a higher purpose but he is not. You are representing the Almighty God on earth to meet a need, solve a problem or answer a question but he is not.

You are on a mission for God but he is not. You have a Father to report to at the end of the day but he has nobody to report to— because nobody sent him to do the evil he does. Remember, you were sent but he was thrown down. At the end of your work on earth, great reward awaits you but eternal destruction awaits the devil. God set joy before you and set grief before him.

The devil already knows the damnation that awaits him at the end of time. Even if he chooses to repent, his repentance is not acceptable to God forever. The fate of the devil is sealed—he is eternally doomed. If you were the devil, God forbid, will you sit down and watch others realize their destinies? Satan is plumbing in the depth of despair. He is not like the façade of an all-powerful being many are made to believe. In fact, this is why he stops at nothing to hinder people from fulfilling God's purpose in their lives.

If there are no thieves, nobody will bother to spend so much on the security system of cars. For the fact that you have an enemy of destiny, you must put in place a destiny security system. Do not live carelessly and expect the devil to watch you become who God intended that you should be and do all He gave you to do.

Consider Paul's exhortation,
Finally, my brethren, be strong in the Lord, and in the power of his might. Put on the whole armour of God, that ye may be able to stand against the wiles of the devil. For we wrestle not against flesh and blood, but against principalities, against powers, against the rulers of the darkness of this world, against spiritual wickedness in high places.
Wherefore take unto you the whole armour of God, that ye may be able to withstand in the evil day, and having done all, to stand. Stand therefore, having your loins girt about with truth, and having on the breastplate of righteousness; And your feet shod with the preparation of the gospel of peace;
Above all, taking the shield of faith, wherewith ye shall be able to quench all the fiery darts of the wicked. And take the helmet of salvation, and the sword of the Spirit, which is the word of God: Praying

always with all prayer and supplication in the Spirit, and watching thereunto with all perseverance and supplication for all saints...
Eph. 6:10-18

In this system, we will consider seven things that will help you withstand every onslaught of hell and realize your destiny in the presence of your enemies. Remember, it is vain to heap goods without security. I have been to the burial of many big men and women who were eliminated by wretched witches in their villages. To become big without divine security is to be a big meat for the hopeless devil and his agents.

My younger brother came and shared with me an early morning revelation of how he saw a meeting of the witches in my village. Their discussion was that, since they could not kill me, they would kill him. He came frightened to his bone and expected me to join him in the fear and pray; but I did not pray. I always tell my family members that no devil is big enough to make me pray in fear.

I simply told my brother, "Just go and do whatsoever I have done that made it impossible for the witches to kill me over the years that they have been trying." From that day, his life has never remained the same and I know that no witch or wizard can come near the dimension of hotness he now has in Christ. I believe nobody can kill you and thus truncate your destiny.

It is your responsibility to put in place an impregnable security system. Every nation is duty bound to build her defence system. Nobody will come from outside to do it. But yours is simple because it only requires your co-operation with God. The Bible says, "...except the LORD keep the city, the watchman waketh but in vain" (Ps. 127:1). With the LORD in the reins, a well-equipped and vigilant watchman will make the difference.

Let the following seven elements among others be available in your security system.

FEET-SHOD

The evil one strikes from the feet—that is where sin gave him access. "And the LORD God said unto the serpent...I will put enmity between thee and the woman, and between thy seed and her seed; it shall bruise thy head, and thou shalt bruise his heel."

Consider his attack on Job,

So went Satan forth from the presence of the LORD, and smote Job with sore boils from the sole of his foot unto his crown. KJV

Satan went out from the presence of the LORD, and struck Job with painful boils from the sole of his foot to the crown of his head. NKJV

So Satan went out from the presence of the LORD, and inflicted loathsome sores on Job from the sole of his foot to the crown of his head. NRSV

Job 2:7

Most instruments of affliction are placed for your feet. We have heard countless stories of people's affliction; the genesis has always been that they stepped on satanic weapons. Similarly, Job's attack started from "...his foot to the crown of his head". The feet of every man, outside God's redemption, is vulnerable to Satan's affliction.

Every satanic stone placed on your way is kept for your foot. When you dash your foot on it, the pains run through your entire body. This is why the LORD promised, "For he shall give his angels charge over thee, to keep thee in all thy ways. They shall bear thee up in their hands, lest thou dash thy foot against a stone" (Ps. 91:11-12).

Satan cannot push you down with your feet intact. To throw you down in any area of your life, he must start from your feet. Have you ever seen this exhortation? "Be not afraid of sudden fear, neither of the desolation of the wicked, when it cometh. For the LORD shall be thy confidence, and shall keep thy foot from being taken" (Prov. 3:25-26).

You see, this is why you need the spiritual shoe for your foot. You cannot achieve speed with a bruised foot. The spiritual shoe is the power of God. Jesus Christ told his disciples, "Behold, I give unto you power to tread on serpents and scorpions, and over all the power of the enemy: and nothing shall by any means hurt you" (Luke 10:19).

If you have your power shoe on, it is possible to step on all instruments of affliction and nothing shall by any means hurt you. Your question might be: How do I get the power to tread on serpents, scorpions and over all the power of the enemy unhurt?

The Bible says,

But as many as received him, to them gave he power to become the sons of God, even to them that believe on his name: Which were born, not of blood, nor of the will of the flesh, nor of the will of man, but of God.

John 1:12-13

The same power that made one God's son renders all the works of the devil ineffective. But I tell you, this is not the funny way people receive Christ nowadays. To truly receive Jesus Christ means to turn away completely from sin (which in the first place made your feet susceptible to the attack of the devil) and totally handover your life to Him.

You have no power to tread on serpents, scorpions and over all the power of the enemy unhurt when you live in sin. Sin is Satan's license to own you and have power over you. The devil can bruise your heel when sin is available in your life. Jesus Christ Himself who was God's first Son on earth said, "...the prince of this world approaches. He has no power over me" (John 14:30 NLT). Do you want to know why? Hear His reply, the devil "hath nothing in me".

Satan holds the advantage over you if he has something in you. The truth is, sin makes you vulnerable to satanic assault. In the race of destiny, bruised heel frustrates speed immeasurably. To receive Jesus Christ in truth means, to turn to God from all your sins and to serve the living and true God (1 Thess. 1:9). It based on this that Isaiah 54:17 finds fulfillment in your life: "No weapon that is formed against thee shall prosper" because you are a servant of the LORD and your righteousness is of Him. It is high time you joined men and women whose feet cannot be bruised and whose speed cannot be frustrated.

The devil can bruise your heel
When sin is available in your life.

SHOCK ABSORBERS

Another very important element of the security system of the speed systems is your shock absorbers. It was Helen Keller who said, "We could never learn to be brave and patient, if there were only joy in the world." Very often we experience joy in our lives but sometimes we find ourselves in a rather shocking situation. It is called life's vicissitudes. There are gallop on the path of destiny you cannot wish away. This aptly explains the imperative of the shock absorbers. They simply reduce the impact of the negative incidents you may encounter.

These shock absorbers are embedded in a virtue called endurance. Let me quickly let you know that endurance is better than what most people define it to be. It is far beyond the ability to bear pain for long. To make your bed with the unpleasant and go nowhere does not speak well of any virtue. Your shock absorbers are not to tie you down but help you out.

Endurance is the virtue that absorbs the shocks and leaves you fit to go forward. It is like the rod of Moses that swallowed the rods of the magicians of Egypt without increase in size. I had driven a car whose front shock absorbers were grounded. I really pitied myself and the car—there was nothing to reduce the impact of distress. Sometimes the body of the car and the tyres will so hit each other that I thought the engine would drop.

There are people that live this way—nothing to absorb the hard impact of the incidents of this life. No one will live long enough to realize his destiny if hundred percent of the effects of life's difficulties are received without mitigation. We cannot count how many people who had met their demise on this account.

Endurance is that security virtue that brings a man out of the terrible gallops of life and move forward as if nothing happened. The LORD taught me a lesson one day that I cannot forget. A hen was going about with her seven chicks and someone drove a car and trampled three of the chicks. I watched to see what the hen would do. To my surprise, she moved away with the remaining four chicks as if nothing had happened.

I said in my heart, "See the stupidity of the hen". But I heard a reply in my spirit, "See the wisdom of the hen". It was not her fault that the chicks were killed. She would not have brought them back to life even if she had cried the entire day. It was wisdom to completely forget the three chicks and run away with the remaining four, and hope for better days. This is endurance.

Consider this,

Dear brothers and sisters, whenever trouble comes your way, let it be an opportunity for joy. For when your faith is tested, your endurance has a chance to grow. So let it grow, for when your endurance is fully developed, you will be strong in character and ready for anything.

James 1:2-4 NLT

It is not all about being able to swim in the sea of pains for a lifetime; it is rather the ability to pull out as soon as possible. What the church had called endurance is what has plagued most adults with blood-afflictions. Endurance is not the ability to sleep in the pain but the strength to get up quickly from it. Some people would have still been alive to pursue God's purpose in their lives if they had not stifled their endurance and crippled their character.

U.S. lawyer, Dean Acheson said, "The manner in which one endures what must be endured is more important than the thing that must be endured." A prominent government official died recently for his inability to absorb the shock of the wife's sudden promiscuity. He was devastated unto death. His manner of endurance only invited stroke and death.

A man with good shock absorbers can be challenged but cannot be devastated. He has all it takes to swallow shocks and expel them immediately. The man of endurance is not the one dying in silence for pains; he is the one that receives pains, releases them quickly to hell where they come from and continue to move with genuine smiles.

Hillary Clinton in referring to her mother-in-law, Virginia Kelley, said, "Virginia's greatest legacy was to show that, even in the midst of personal trials and pain, you can and must keep going. Her lesson was that, no matter how hard life gets, you get up in the morning, say a prayer, put a smile on your face and go out and brave the world to do the best you can."

For me, I see the shocks in life as well pumped balls, and I constitute myself as a wall to them. They can hit me but they are not permitted to stay more than a split second. They must fall off while I remain stronger and progressive. It is this type of endurance that guarantees the realization of destiny.

The Bible says,

We can rejoice, too, when we run into problems and trials, for we know that they are good for us—they help us learn to endure. And endurance develops strength of character in us, and character strengthens our confident expectation of salvation.

Rom. 5:3-5 NLT

Jesus Christ said, "...he that endureth to the end shall be saved" (Matt. 10:22). Remember, the endurance that gets to THE END is not the one that facilitates illness and death halfway into your destiny journey. The shock absorbers in your car are not to keep your car grounded in the potholes but to come out and move forward as if nothing happened.

If the road is rough and your shock absorbers are bad, you will be limited in speed. So, your endurance is a security for both your existence and speed.

Some people live with pains
While others resend them to hell.

SEAT BELT

Of what favour is it to the Road Safety Commission that you use the seat belt while driving? It is solely for your own safety. Have you ever asked, "Why did the designers of car add seat belts?" Why does the Road Safety Commission fine people a substantial sum of money for failing to use the seat belt?"

You see, as you drive on the path of destiny, the messengers of Satan are detailed to buffet you. Paul the apostle said, "...there was given to me a thorn in the flesh, the messenger of Satan to buffet me..." (2 Cor. 12:7). Even the Lord Jesus Christ was hurt, embarrassed, and treated unkindly on the path of destiny.

The Bible says,

And some began to spit on him, and to cover his face, and to buffet him, and to say unto him, Prophesy: and the servants did strike him with the palms of their hands.

Mark 14:65

On the path of destiny, you will certainly encounter moments of great shaking and your only need will be to be held. This is where and when you need the belt of truth. When satanic storms come to push you down, the belt of truth will hold you firmly. Many people have been displaced from their destiny positions and seats for not putting on the belt of truth that the Lord has provided.

Many marriages and ministries have been destroyed because the operators neglected the girdle of truth. Many great businesses and establishments crumbled because their managers took the belt of truth for granted. When the messengers of Satan pounce on them, they had nothing to hold them. There are satanic storms you cannot withstand if you are not held by the girdle of truth.

The Bible says,

So put on God's armor now! Then when the evil day comes, you will be able to resist the enemy's attacks; and after fighting to the end, you will still hold your ground. So stand ready, with truth as a belt tight around your waist...

Eph. 6:13-14 TEV

The knowledge and the exhibition of the truth are the ways to fasten your belt of truth. You need to know the truth, which is "...every word that proceedeth out of the mouth of the LORD..." (Deut. 8:3). You can never be free from the wickedness of the devil without the good knowledge of the truth.

Hear this,

Then said Jesus to those Jews which believed on him, If ye continue in my word, then are ye my disciples indeed; And ye shall know the truth, and the truth shall make you free.

John 8:31-32

There are many facts in the world but they are never securities for your destiny. The Word of God, who is God—even Jesus Christ our Lord, who is the truth, is the security for your destiny. He said, "I am the way, the truth, and the life..." You see, the more you know Jesus Christ—the truth, the more inconsequential the devil becomes to you and the more helpless he becomes towards you.

You also need to exhibit the truth daily. God wants you to live out the truth in every way. Anything that reveals a lie in your life brings you under the devil. No matter how well you tell lies, you cannot exceed the devil. "He... abode not in the truth, because there is no truth in him. When he speaketh a lie, he speaketh of his own: for he is a liar, and the father of it" (John 8:44).

It is a great security measure to constantly speak the truth, live the truth and be a witness of the truth. Satan is helpless when he cannot get you to speak a lie, live a lie and witness to a lie. You must know that God is pleased when you have on your belt of truth. He "...desirest truth in the inward parts..." (Ps. 51:6). No devil can stop your speed when truth is the belt that holds you in life.

The Father is the God of truth. The Son is the truth. The Holy Ghost is the Spirit of truth. You need to be a man of truth to join the trinity of truth and thus enjoy maximum security. Remember, no aircraft takes off without the counsel, "fasten your seatbelt". On a daily basis, there are some people who are paid via your taxes to stand in the sun and rain just to ensure that you use your seat belt.

If you are on the path of destiny and want to achieve speed unimpeded, accept my counsel, fasten your belt of truth.

When all you need is to be held,
Live the truth.

FIRE EXTINGUISHER

On the scale of value, certain things may appear trivial but they are as important as the things we value the most when the need for them arises. From our car analogy, fire extinguisher is a clear example of this. It is rarely used on a daily basis but when the need for it calls, it is like a knight in shining armour – it comes to your rescue. To stay on the straight course of your destiny and enjoy speed unhindered, fire extinguisher, which symbolizes faith, is a prerequisite.

You need to realize that the enemy is working around the clock to stop you from fulfilling your destiny; therefore, hold on to faith – your impregnable defence tool against all that the enemy throws at you. The fierceness of the fire against you is not as important as the capacity of your fire extinguisher – faith. Faith can take on anything.

The Bible says,

Above all, taking the shield of faith, wherewith ye shall be able to quench all the fiery darts of the wicked. And take the helmet of salvation, and the sword of the Spirit, which is the word of God...

Eph. 6:16-17

Faith has the quenching power. With it, you "shall be able to quench ALL the fiery darts of the wicked". With it, you shall be able to put out satanic fire set to your destiny. There is no activity of the devil you cannot overcome if you have faith.

Look at this,

For whatsoever is born of God overcometh the world: and this is the victory that overcometh the world, even our faith.

1 John 5:4

The greatest disfavour you can do yourself is to live within faith. It is actually impossible to live at all without faith. Faith guarantees your life and without it, you are but a piece of meat in the mouth of the enemy. The "fiery darts of the wicked" are so numerous against a man's mind for him to survive without faith. Faith is the quenches of all forms of satanic darts. Faith is one of the most powerful forces that operate on the earth. The stories of great overcomers start with "By faith..." (Hebrews 11).

Many people "...through faith subdued kingdoms, wrought righteousness, obtained promises, stopped the mouths of lions, quenched the violence of fire, escaped the edge of the sword, out of weakness were made strong, waxed valiant in fight, turned to flight the armies of the aliens" (Heb. 11:33-34). As far as destiny is concerned, you have "the violence of fire" you will always quench.

I do not see how you can win in this world without faith. Destiny-fight is meant for your faith. This is why it is called the "fight of faith" (1 Tim. 6:12). If you are not ready to fight with the quenching power of your faith, the violence of satanic fire will eliminate you too quickly. You need to get the fire extinguisher of the force of your faith always ready to quench any spark of devilish fire.

You cannot stop the devil from making fire,
And he cannot stop you from quenching it by faith.

SHARPER-SWORD

Faith is total reliance on God's Word. No Word of God, no faith. The Word is the real quencher of evil fires. With your reliance on the Word, you can bring to naught all of the devil's assaults, both of force and fraud, all the deceits he pushes into your mind and all the snares he lays for you.

You remember that Jesus Christ resisted all the advances of the devil with "It is written..." and he won. Consider this text most diligently. "Then was Jesus led up of the Spirit into the wilderness to be tempted of the devil. And when he had fasted forty days and forty nights, he was afterward an hungred. And when the tempter came to him, he said, If thou be the Son of God, command that these stones be made bread. But he answered and said, It is written, Man shall not live by bread alone, but by every word that proceedeth out of the mouth of God.

Then the devil taketh him up into the holy city, and setteth him on a pinnacle of the temple, And saith unto him, If thou be the Son of God, cast thyself down: for it is written, He shall give his angels charge concerning thee: and in their hands they shall bear thee up, lest at any time thou dash thy foot against a stone. Jesus said unto him, It is written again, Thou shalt not tempt the Lord thy God.

Again, the devil taketh him up into an exceeding high mountain, and sheweth him all the kingdoms of the world, and the glory of them; And saith unto him, All these things will I give thee, if thou wilt fall down and worship me. Then saith Jesus unto him, Get thee hence, Satan: for it is written, Thou shalt worship the Lord thy God, and him only shalt thou serve. Then the devil leaveth him, and, behold, angels came and ministered unto him" (Matt. 4:1-11).

You have no other way of quenching the devil's darts; you need to follow Christ's footstep of "It is written..." The Bible says, "For even hereunto were ye called: because Christ also suffered for us, leaving us an example, that ye should follow his steps..." (1 Peter 2:21). No matter the kind of fire the enemy kindles, there is a Word meant to quench it.

There is therefore no satanic flame you cannot quench. Only let your faith pump the relevant Word of God against it. There are people who travel with an empty cylinder of fire extinguisher in their car just to keep up the pretence of obeying government's regulation. What they failed to understand is that laws are meant to ensure the security of life, and to flout them flagrantly is to put life and destiny is jeopardy.

There are people who claim to have faith in God but do not hold to any of His promises. You see, determination does not equal faith. The cylinder of your faith must always be full of the Word. When you press your faith, let the enemy hear the Word of God and your victory is sure. Never have faith for decoration; have it for the demonstration of "the power of God" (1 Cor. 2:5).

The Bible says,

Where the word of a king is, there is power: and who may say unto him, What doest thou?

Eccl. 8:4

For the word of God is quick, and powerful...

Heb. 4:12,

The voice of the LORD is powerful; the voice of the LORD is full of majesty.

Ps. 29:4

With your Word-filled faith, you are fully equipped to quench any "violence of fire" and to continue your destiny journey unhindered.

Always reply the wicked one with "it is written".

AIR-BAGS

Some years ago, a car had an accident in front of my office in the night. On getting there in the morning, I was captivated by three white materials that were said to have shut out spontaneously during the accident from the car's board and stood between the driver and the shattered windscreen. Even though the car I drove then had air-bags, I got to know something about the air-bags and their safety function for the first time that day. Oh! How thoughtful and safety mindful are some car designers! Something is built inside of your car to spontaneously respond to danger of its own.

Whether the car designers know it or not; they have copied God's design in every true believer in Christ. If you believe in the Lord Jesus Christ, you have the gift of an air-bag in you called righteousness. It is God's gift to you for receiving Jesus Christ as your Lord and personal Saviour. You do nothing extra to have it; it is the gift of God.

The Bible says,

For if by one man's offence death reigned by one; much more they which receive abundance of grace and of the gift of righteousness shall reign in life by one, Jesus Christ.

Rom. 5:17

You are the righteousness of God in Christ. "For he hath made him to be sin for us, who knew no sin; that we might be made the righteousness of God in him" (2 Cor. 5:21). You make effort towards holiness but not unto righteousness. You are made the righteousness of God in Christ. And as the air-bags, you cannot see this righteousness but it is in you with a proactive setting—sure, it responds before hurt gets to you.

This is why,

No weapon that is formed against thee shall prosper; and every tongue that shall rise against thee in judgment thou shalt condemn. This is the heritage of the servants of the LORD, and their righteousness is of me, saith the LORD.

Isaiah 54:17

You see, anything can happen to you if the gift of righteousness is not in you. Paul the apostle likened righteousness to the breastplate that covers the entire chest region of a soldier. This is the most sensitive region of a man's life and there righteousness is on duty. Is it good to pursue the realization of your destiny with your seat of life exposed? You know it is not good.

If there is anything you need to go and get immediately, it is the gift of righteousness. You can get it now by accepting Jesus Christ as your Lord and personal Saviour. If nobody can bring you down, moving forward is certain.

Righteousness confuses the devil about you.

HEAD-COVER

You will never be a victim in the race of destiny in Jesus' Name. I sincerely want you to take seriously the security system of the speed systems. There is nothing to pride yourself about if you take off for your journey in grand style only to be grounded by the enemy few kilometers from home. It is wisdom, a great one at that, to be security conscious.

This is the wisdom attributed to conies by the writer of Proverbs chapter thirty. The Bible says, "There be four things which are little upon the earth, but they are exceeding wise: The ants are a people not strong, yet they prepare their meat in the summer; The conies are but a feeble folk, yet make they their houses in the rocks..." (Prov. 30:24-28).

The conies know that they are weak compared to the hunters that are after them. They make up their minds never to live in a way that would let anybody kill them anyhow. They look for places that will be difficult or impossible for the hunters to reach them. They consider the rocks most reliable and they make their houses in them.

The Bible says,

Cliff badgers: delicate little animals who protect themselves by living among the rocks.

Prov. 30:24 TLB

You must know that your life is delicate and that a brutish adversary looks for it. You are exhorted, "Be sober, be vigilant; because your adversary the devil, as a roaring lion, walketh about, seeking whom he may devour..." (1 Peter 5:8). Why not make up your mind like the conies never to live in a way that would let anybody kill you anyhow.

The conies are safe in the rocks and you too will be safe in the Rock. Their safety is in the physical rocks but your Rock is the Person of God.

For who is God save the LORD? or who is a rock save our God?

Ps. 18:31, 2 Sam. 22:32

The conies' wisdom is to live in the rocks—places impossible for the killers to reach. This is the same experience for all those who are truly in Christ. They are in the Rock no devil can penetrate. Their lives are "...hid with Christ in God" (Col. 3:3). This is "...the secret place of the most High..." that you need to dwell perpetually.

The truth is, you will remain under satanic grip if you are not in Christ. You are not safe if you are not saved. You are not secure outside the Saviour. As the breastplate covers the soldier's chest region, so the helmet of salvation covers your head. In this wicked world, you are a victim waiting to happen if you pursue your destiny with unprotected head.

Salvation is the best security lock for your life. No man can steal or kill a saved soul. Jesus Christ said, "My sheep hear my voice, and I know them, and they follow me: And I give unto them eternal life; and they shall never perish, neither shall any man pluck them out of my hand. My Father, which gave them me, is greater than all; and no man is able to pluck them out of my Father's hand" (John 10:27-29).

Please, be saved to be safe. Jesus Christ Himself told Nicodemus that he needed to "be born again" (John 3:3). You too need to be born-again to be safe in life. Do not be like the achievers that died like fowls in the hands of some tiny witches. Secure divine security—be born again. To be born again does not mean to be socially irrelevant; it means to give your life totally to Jesus Christ. This is what you can do right now.

If you want to give your life to Christ, say this prayer: Lord Jesus, I come to you as a sinner. I appreciate your death on the cross for me. I receive you today as my Lord and personal Saviour. Please, forgive my sins and cleanse me by your blood. Thank you, Jesus! Today, I am saved. I am now born-again. Amen.

May God give you the grace for the race.

www.ingramcontent.com/pod-product-compliance
Lightning Source LLC
Chambersburg PA
CBHW052127150726
48002CB00006B/2510